A BOOK OF
WAYSIDE FRUITS

By Margaret McKenny
and Edith F. Johnston

A BOOK OF WILD FLOWERS
A BOOK OF GARDEN FLOWERS
A BOOK OF WAYSIDE FRUITS

A Book of
WAYSIDE FRUITS

by MARGARET McKENNY
and EDITH F. JOHNSTON

NEW YORK · THE MACMILLAN COMPANY · 1945

Lithographed in the United States of America by William C. D. Glaser, New York

Dedicated by
the Author and Artist
to *Eva S. Troy*
keen observer of wayside beauty
and to
Lillian Gerard Glaser
for her invaluable encouragement
and assistance

FOREWORD

Every year, from early June until frost, the bounty of wayside fruits is set forth on bush and tree and earth for the nourishment and delight of the birds. They are greedy banqueters, too, often devouring all the fruit of some favorite sort before any of it is ripe. The shadblow is the earliest to be so consumed, as its rosy little apples are ready for the bird table first of all, and are eagerly relished by both adults and fledglings. Wild strawberries, all warmed and sweetened by the sun, are delectable morsels, not to the birds alone, but to ants and mice and men. Pin-cherries, choke-cherries, rum-cherries are appreciated by bird and man alike. The warm days of the year are enriched by a continuous procession of luscious small fruits, flashing out like jewels in the green thickets for their brief season, and disappearing to give place to the next tempting course. As autumn approaches, the hips and haws and the berries of the many dogwoods begin to glow with color and in the swamp, winterberry, spicebush and Jack-in-the-pulpit are aflame with their fire-red berries.

After frost has touched the woods and fields and ended the lovely pageant of flower and leaf, many of the wild fruits remain and furnish food for the birds when snow covers the ground. Black haw, high-bush cranberry, maple-leaved viburnum, and many others, neglected while more palatable dainties were to be had, now are hailed with delight by hungry birds, face to face with a season of scarcity before the next feast is spread.

One of the happiest features of a winter's walk is the memory of the drifts of sweet blossom and glowing fruit which covered these bare shrubs in spring and summer, and will cover them again when winter is past. Here stand the blueberry bushes, waiting to be decorated afresh with their tiny urns, pink-tinted and scallop-edged, here the flowering dogwood holds up its soft-gray four-square packets, awaiting its time to open out into glorious white bract and chartreuse blossom, here the slim bare twigs of the spicebush are knobbed with their scale-covered buds which hold within them all the fragrance of the April wood.

> "The north cannot undo them,
> With a sleety whistle through them;
> Nor frozen thawings glue them
> From budding at the prime."*

Here beauty was; here it will be again. Blossomtime, seedtime and harvest shall not fail.

Out of all the teeming abundance of this wayside bounty a mere handful of specimens has been chosen to serve as examples of the beauty and lavishness of the wild fruit harvest. Preference has been given to those most commonly seen and admired. Probably all of the fruits here represented will be familiar to every nature-lover. All might well be cultivated in hedgerow or garden as an invitation to the migrant birds, to add the loveliness of flight and song to that of color and fragrance.

EDITH FARRINGTON JOHNSTON

*Keats: *Stanzas,* from Posthumous and Fugitive Poems.

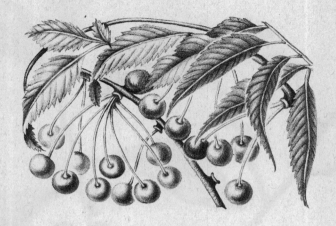

EARLY SUMMER

Spicebush

Jack-in-the-Pulpit

Shadbush

Wild Black Cherry

Wild Rose

Strawberry

American Elderberry and Red Elderberry

Trumpet Honeysuckle

Black cap Raspberry

Highbush Blueberry

Flowering Raspberry

Edith F. Johnston

Spicebush

In late summer the fruits of the spicebush hang from the branches like drops of glowing red sealing wax. The yellow-fleshed fruit has the same aromatic taste as the twigs and new leaves, which are so delightful to nibble on in the early spring.

Birds of the edge of the woodland eat the red fruits. The veery, with his whispered descending spiral of song, feeds the juicy scarlet drops to his young, and the slender gray catbird, with his mocking call, acts as if the harvest should be his alone.

We find the spice-bush on the edges of the swamps, in damp open woods, or often bending over little streams. It seldom grows more than ten feet in height and has many branches from the ground. The slender, brittle twigs make a delicate intertwined pattern, especially lovely when outlined with feathery snow. In March or April, before there is a leaf on the protecting trees, the branches are set thick with tiny yellow flowers, like a golden mist against the pale springtime sky.

The oval, sharp-pointed leaves unroll soon after the flowers appear. They are pale green at first, then in summer become dull green above and lighter below. In the early autumn the foliage turns a clear buttercup yellow, brightening the borders of the woodland and the margins of the streams like bands of sunshine.

Jack-in-the-pulpit

On the edge of the marshy woods or in the rich black soil near the brook, in late summer, we find the red, club-shaped clusters of Jack-in-the-pulpit fruits. The large three-parted leaves and the sheltering sheath have withered and fallen away, but the stalk which was the Jack in the springtime is now top-heavy with oval fruits so intensely red and glossy that they almost dazzle the eyes. As these fruits ripen and fall away the blackish purple core shows, marked with white scars.

In early spring the furled foliage of the Jack-in-the-pulpit pushes through the covering of last autumn's leaves. Above the green or purple flower stalk is a drooping canopy striped pale and dark green, or green and purple.

The turnip-shaped root is burning and acrid if eaten raw; but the Indians used both berries and root for food, first boiling them to destroy the fiery taste.

The Jack-in-the-pulpit belongs to the Arum Family and has many relatives, which we may know by the central stalk called the spadix and the sheathing leaf called the spathe. Among these are the skunk cabbage, the calla lily, and the Krubi, which has a bloom taller than a man—the largest bloom of any plant in the world.

13

Edith F. Johnston

Shadbush

The small, rosy purple, applelike fruits of the shadbush cluster on the branches in early summer. They are delicious to eat; but we seldom get a taste, for the birds are always first at the feast.

More than forty kinds of birds eagerly eat the little apples or take them away to their thirsty nestlings. They are the favorite food of the brilliant scarlet tanager and the sleek, fawn-colored cedar waxwing.

Though it often grows like a shrub, the shadbush sometimes becomes a slender, high-branched tree with a smooth, silver-brown bark. The five-petaled flowers and the tiny apples show that it belongs to the Rose Family. The delicate white blossoms wreathe the branches in early spring. They seem to float like clouds of mist under the leafless trees. Fleeting as April snow, they are here today and gone tomorrow.

The early settlers in the Eastern states gave this tree the name of shadbush, or shadblow, because it blooms when the shad run up the rivers to spawn. In other parts of the country it is called Juneberry. In the West there is a species called serviceberry. In the mountains it often fruits so heavily that the branches are bent low with the clusters of red and blue fruits.

The juicy berries of the shadbush were food for the Indians, who ate them fresh or dried them for the winter.

Edith F. Johnston

Wild Black Cherry

Ripening in late summer or early fall, the long sprays of dark purple fruit of the wild cherry hang from the branches. Even before the fruit is ripe the tree is full of a host of hungry birds, bright tanagers and orioles chattering excitedly in competition with rose-breasted grosbeaks and blue jays. This tree is one of the most valuable to have in the bird sanctuary, for nearly a hundred kinds of birds are known to eat the fruit.

In the forest wild black cherries often reach over a hundred feet in height with a strong, straight trunk covered with dark brown bark, the inner layers of which are bitter and aromatic. In less favorable situations the trunk may be short and the boughs widespread and twisted. Sometimes it grows with its roots wedged in the surf-sprayed rocks of the New England coast and then, because of its struggle with the storms and cold, it is gnarled and stunted.

In the spring the unfolding leaves are wine-colored, then later become dark green and very glossy. The foliage, especially when the branches are broken from the tree and the leaves are withered, is poisonous to cattle.

The wild black cherry belongs to the Rose Family and its white, almond-scented blossoms have five petals. In late spring every branch is draped with the long, drooping sprays of bloom, which make a charming combination with the purplish red of the young leaves.

Edith F. Johnston

Wild Rose

In every part of our country the crimson or orange fruits of the wild rose brighten the roadsides and the fields. The fruit is called a hip and is a fleshy, hollow cup packed full of seeds. A jam with a delicate rose flavor and perfume is made from the fruits after the seeds have been removed.

In the Eastern states the rose hips cling to the branches all through the winter, and when snow covers the ground they become the food of many birds. Both the bobwhite and the ruffed grouse burst through the snowbanks and feed upon them.

The frail five-petaled flowers, shading from pale pink to deep rose in the many different species, open from day to day all summer. In the East and South wild roses grow in the open fields or on the edge of swamps. On the prairies of the Middle West and in the thickets and hedgerows of the eastern states grows the Prairie Rose, our only climbing wild rose. In the mountains and in the Pacific states, acres of wild roses border the lakes and the shores of the ocean. In many parts of the West the sweetbrier rose of Scotland has gone wild, and after every summer shower the air is filled with the fragrance of its aromatic foliage. During the soft, rainy winter days, the ring-necked pheasant and the California quail fatten comfortably on the orange hips.

Edith F. Johnston

Wild Strawberry

In June the unplowed meadows are often dyed red with the little wild strawberry. The dainty, fragrant fruits are held on slender, arching stems above the velvety, three-parted leaves. The fruit is small, but within that tiny crimson globe is held the perfume, the very essence, of a glowing June day.

The wild strawberry grows in many parts of America. In the Eastern states we find it in the open meadows among the dandelions and oxeye daisies. Often, too, it grows along a woodland path where the bright red fruit is shadowed by the drooping fronds of ferns. On the Western prairies the strawberry plants grow in wide patches and the delicious berries nestle close, hidden by the tufted grasses or by their own deceiving scarlet leaves.

The strawberry flower, with its five pure white petals, looks like a wild rose and shows us that the strawberry belongs to the Rose Family, which has given us so many of our fruits.

Both children and birds welcome strawberry time. We often see a busy mother robin hurrying to her babies with a crimson berry in her beak. The gay meadowlark makes his covered nest in open fields where the wild strawberry is close at hand for his hungry brood.

Edith F. Johnston

American Elderberry and
Red Elderberry

In August the heavy-headed clusters of the American elderberry hang low over the stone fences which border the lanes of the Eastern states. All through the Middle West also, where the vast cornfields wave under the blazing sun, elderberry bushes along the highway give food to the hungry birds. The berrylike fruits are dark purple with crimson juice. They are borne in large flat clusters and are often used for jam and jelly.

In June the bushes are covered with a foam of white blossoms with a pleasant perfume. Each cluster is made up of hundreds of tiny five-parted flowers.

A lover of the shaded mountain ravine, the red elderberry ripens its fruit early in the summer. The shining scarlet clusters are shaped like pyramids and, on the edge of the stream, tumbling down through the hemlock grove, glow like flames against the dark green. In the mountains of the West we often see the brilliant fruit with a background of snow-covered peaks. There the fruit is eaten eagerly by flocks of band-tailed pigeons.

The red elderberry blooms early in the spring. The small creamy white flowers are wheel-shaped and have a rather disagreeable odor.

The foliage of both shrubs is feather-form. The leaf of the American elderberry has from five to eleven leaflets, and that of the red from five to seven.

Trumpet Honeysuckle

Such a glowing orange-red that they seem translucent, the fruits of the trumpet honeysuckle gleam on the high-climbing vines at the end of summer. Though often cultivated, the vines seem to grow more luxuriantly in the tangled thicket or when draping themselves over some half-dead tree than when they are trained carefully over a trellis in the garden. We find the vines all through the woodlands from Connecticut to Florida and west to Texas.

The smooth oval leaves are dull blue-green above and silvery beneath. They grow opposite each other on the stem and the two upper ones are joined just below the flower stem, making a little green saucer for the bloom.

The long, trumpet-shaped flowers are deep scarlet or orange without and golden-yellow within. At the base of the trumpet is a store of nectar; and hummingbirds flash from flower to flower, pausing only long enough to plunge their long bills to the bottom of the blossoms.

Edith F. Johnston

Blackcap Raspberry

The arching stems of the blackcap bend gracefully toward the ground near boulders in the open fields or along old stone walls. The fruit of the blackcap is not one berry. It is a dense cluster of tiny fruits called drupes, each one surrounding a central seed. This cluster fits like a cap over a white base, and when ripe it is easily lifted off. That is why this raspberry is called blackcap.

The new stems of the blackcap are a soft shade of purplish lavender covered with a white powdery substance called bloom. The root of the blackcap lives on from year to year; but every summer after the fruit is ripe, last year's stalks become brown and die, and new stalks are sent out to take their place. Often the tips of the stalks arch to the ground and there take root, forming new plants.

The leaves are divided into three, or sometimes five, leaflets and are silvery underneath. They do not change color in the autumn, but wither and fall with the first frost.

The flowers grow in clusters and the five frail white petals soon fall away from the golden center of pistils and stamens. Then the raspberry is formed, first green, then red, finally purple-black, sweet and juicy. As these fruits give food to more than a hundred kinds of birds, the blackcap is valuable on the border of the bird sanctuary.

Highbush Blueberry

In late July or August the slender branches of the highbush blueberry, sometimes called the swamp blueberry, are loaded with the delicious fruit. If the bushes grow in marshy ground in the open woods, they often reach higher than a man's head; but when they grow in the dry open fields, they are seldom more than waist-high.

Sometimes the juicy berries are blue with a pearly white bloom; sometimes they are a shining black. They can always be distinguished from huckleberries because their seeds are so fine that we hardly notice them as we eat the fruit, while huckleberries have hard little nutlike seeds. Some bushes have large sweet berries, while another bush near by may have small acid fruit. Wild blueberries are gathered every year for the market, and selected varieties with large sweet berries are grown in the garden.

Hosts of birds eat blueberries. The robins, thrushes, quails, and ruffed grouse depend upon them for food all through the summer.

In May or June the blueberry is covered with drooping clusters of little white or pink bells, very like those of the lily-of-the-valley. In autumn the foliage turns to deep rose and purplish red, making notes of warm color in the fields or by the roadside where the bushes have been planted in drifts along our open highways.

Edith F. Johnston.

14370

Flowering Raspberry

Fortunately for the birds the velvety red fruit of the flowering raspberry has very little flavor to make it attractive to us. Flowers blossom and fruits ripen all summer. The Baltimore oriole, in his glowing livery of orange and black, and the sweetly singing rose-breasted grosbeak are always able to find the sharply acid raspberries for food and drink for their nestlings.

Along the moist and shady mountain trail or on the edge of a cool woodland path, the flowering raspberry often grows in dense masses. The young shoots are velvety with thickly growing red hairs. Later the main stems are covered with a thin, shreddy bark.

The rough, hairy leaves are broad, sometimes nearly a foot across, and are shaped very much like those of the maple. They remain green until the frost withers them in the autumn.

The round flower buds are covered with the green calyx, which tassels out from the center in five points. The fragrant blossoms with their five petals are deep rose-purple but soon become faded. New blossoms open day by day, looking like small wild roses set here and there amidst the luxuriant foliage.

Edith F. Johnston

MIDSUMMER

Wild Blackberry

White and Red Baneberry

Carrion-flower

Climbing or Bittersweet Nightshade

Pokeweed

Japanese Honeysuckle

Snowberry and Indian Currant

Red Osier Dogwood

American Bittersweet or Waxwork

Sassafras

Silky Dogwood

Wild Blackberry

The glinting fruits of the wild blackberry twinkle at us from the edge of old abandoned fields, the stalks coming up in thickets in the grass and ferns. In shadier spots, near the edge of the woods, the blackberries are larger and juicier but not so sweet as those which grow in the full sunshine.

Although we say "blackberries," the fruits are not true berries but clusters of little fruits called drupes, each one containing a hard seed and all clinging fast to a central hard core, the cluster when ripe separating easily from the calyx.

The tall, spiny stalks make it difficult for us to gather the juicy fruits but form no barrier for the flitting birds, and blackberry season is a time of plenty for hundreds of them. The flame-red cardinal and his soberly clad brown mate bring their youngsters to the source of supplies, while the chewink and quail slip through the prickly stalks gathering their share from the ripe fruit which falls to the ground.

The white, five-petaled blossoms wreathe the branches early in June. If the bees scatter the golden pollen from flower to flower, there will be a plentiful crop later in the summer. Then, if we dare to defy the thorns, we can claim a share from the birds.

In autumn the foliage of the blackberry turns to deep purplish red or crimson, and we can often locate a patch for next summer by watching for this rich glowing color.

Edith F. Johnston

White and Red Baneberry

Growing in the rich leaf mold of shady woods, in midsummer, the top-heavy clusters of the white baneberry stand out against the dark shadows. The oval fruits are white with a dark spot and are held on the fruit stalk with *thick* rose-red stems.

The red baneberry is found in shady woods, also, but grows more profusely farther north than does the white baneberry. The gleaming red berries are attached to the stalk with *slender* green stems, and ripen several weeks earlier than the fruit of the white.

In the woodland, baneberry customarily stands from two to three feet high—the white usually higher. It is easily transplanted and takes kindly to a shady corner of the garden, where it often grows larger than in the wild and has longer clusters of berries. Both plants have compound leaves; that is, leaves cut up into many small leaflets.

Both baneberries belong to the Buttercup Family and the flowers of the two plants are similar — fluffy clusters of narrow creamy white petals and pale greenish pistils and stamens. The red baneberry blooms first, its feathery blossoms opening under the leafless trees with the flowers of the bloodroot and Dutchman's breeches, and the white baneberry shows its creamy plumes just as the fruits of the red are forming.

Edith F. Johnston

Carrion Flower

Stretching its lithe length in the sunshine like a great lazy cat, the vine of the carrion flower lies along the top of the old stone walls in the secluded lanes and byways of the greater part of the Northeastern states. The bluish black berries are crowded together in such tight clusters that they form a ball. These round clusters of fruit, on long stems, are held on the vines nearly all winter, and will remain firm for several months if brought into the house for a winter bouquet.

Although the carrion flower belongs to the Lily Family, which gives us so many lovely and fragrant garden flowers, it is an outcast from our gardens because the clusters of little, six-parted greenish blossoms have a very disagreeable odor. This odor is disgusting to us but attracts certain insects which carry the pollen from one vine to another, for the flowers which become berries are on a separate vine from those which bear the pollen.

So, far from man's ordered garden, where flowers must have either beauty or a pleasant fragrance, the carrion flowers grow lustily, ripening their fruits in late August. Soon the migrating thrushes will discover them or the robin and catbird will add them to their list of autumn fruits.

Later in the fall the oval leaves, with their heart-shaped bases, will turn deep orange and russet red, clinging to the green, thornless vines until long after many of the trees are leafless.

Climbing or Bittersweet Nightshade

In late summer and early fall the scarlet berries of the false bittersweet hang from the graceful vines.

The false bittersweet belongs to the Deadly Nightshade Family and, though this family gives us such valuable food plants as the potato, the tomato, and the pepper, the oval red berries are poisonous. If we look closely at the little purple flowers with their pointed clusters of stamens, we can see how much they look like the wheel-shaped blossoms of the potato. The lower leaves are oval; the upper ones have two or three earlike lobes.

All through the country the false bittersweet grows along shady hedgerows or in rather marshy woodlands. It grows especially well near a river, draping itself in festoons from boughs hanging over the water. Often in September we find both purple flowers and scarlet fruit set together among leaves which have bleached to a soft shade of heliotrope.

No one knows just when the false bittersweet was brought to America from the Old World. Perhaps one of the Pilgrim mothers brought a few seeds and planted them in the rocky New England soil, hoping they would grow and twine over her log cabin and remind her of her cottage in England. But now the vine has made this country its home, and we find it growing from the Eastern states to the far West coast.

Edith F. Johnston

Pokeweed

In tangled thickets by the roadside, or in waste corners of the farmyard, grow the vigorous plants of the pokeberry. The long smooth stalks sometimes reach above ten feet and are often cerise or crimson in color. The fruiting stalks are bent with the weight of the sprays of dark purple berries. These berries have a rich red juice, which was once used by country children for red ink and for dyeing. The seeds of the fruit are poisonous.

The leaves are large, pointed and oval in shape, bright yellow-green, and spotted as if they were stained with purple-red wine. The flowers have no petals; they have only a row of white or pinkish sepals around the flat green center, which will become the berry.

The whole plant of the pokeberry dies to the ground in the fall, the root living on from year to year. The root is poisonous, but the tender new shoots are often gathered and cooked like asparagus. Great care should always be taken not to cut any of the root if the young sprouts are gathered for food.

Though the pokeberry once grew only along the edge of the woodland, it has now become a weed in many places in the Eastern states. Even in Europe, where it was taken many years ago, it has escaped from the garden and is found along the country roads.

Few wild fruits are more eagerly eaten by the birds than those of the pokeberry. One of the common names of this plant is the pigeonberry, because the wild pigeons are so fond of the berries.

Edith F. Johnston

Japanese Honeysuckle

Forming a tangled mass along many of our highways and often hanging in great draperies from the trees, we see the Japanese honeysuckle, a climbing shrub with shiny black berries.

This honeysuckle was brought to America from Asia over a hundred years ago, and now has made itself thoroughly at home in many of the Eastern and Southern states. It grows so rampantly in many regions that it has killed out and taken the place of more delicate and beautiful native vines and shrubs, completely smothering the smaller wild flowers.

This honeysuckle is quite useful when planted on steep banks, to hold the soil, or on a fence to make a shelter in a bird sanctuary, but great care should be taken not to allow it to escape to the woodland.

The fragrant, two-lipped flowers, growing in pairs, are at first pure white, then change to yellow. The fruit is eaten by the birds and, as the foliage is almost evergreen, the vines form a good winter shelter when growing near the feeding station. Whenever possible, however, a native plant, such as the glossy-leaved evergreen bearberry, should be used for the purpose instead of this profusely growing climber from the Orient.

Edith F. Johnston

Snowberry and Indian Currant

Its slender branches often bowed with the weight of the clusters of little white balls, the snowberry grows along the rocky hillside or the banks of rivers. In the mountains of the West it often fruits so profusely that it seems as if there were drifts of snow along the side of the railroad embankments. So charming are the waxy white fruits, especially after the leaves have fallen in the autumn, that the snowberry is often used in the garden.

The bright green, oval leaves grow opposite each other on the twigs. The small, bell-shaped flowers, white or a delicate pink in color, grow in clusters. They open one by one through the summer, so there are often fruit and flowers on the bush at the same time.

Both the Indian currant and the snowberry belong to the Honeysuckle Family. The branches of the Indian currant are like slender wands and the flowers, small greenish bells filled with nectar, grow from the point where the opposite leaves join the stem. They bloom in August and are soon followed by dense clusters of purplish red berries which show brightly when the foliage withers. These purple-skinned, white-fleshed fruits stay long on the branches unharmed by frost. They are so tasteless that even the birds neglect them; so they cling to the branches all winter.

Edith F. Johnston

Red Osier Dogwood

The flat clusters of the round, white, or lead-colored fruits of the red osier dogwood are found on the bushes late in summer. Like the fruits of other trees and shrubs of the Dogwood Family, their discovery is always a delightful event to the birds. The brown thrasher, who nests in the tangled shrubbery on the edge of the woods, shares them with his cousin, the saucy catbird. Many other birds eat them also, for the osier dogwood is found all across the country, even as far west as British Columbia.

The red osier blooms in June. The cream-white flowers with downy stems are in small flat clusters. Each flower has four petals and four stamens; and so we can always tell it from the viburnum, which has five-parted starry flowers with five stamens.

The pointed leaves, growing opposite each other on the twigs, are at first reddish and covered with silvery hairs; then in summer they are bright green above and downy below. In autumn they turn to deep crimson brightened with touches of orange and yellow.

The osier dogwood's time of greatest charm is in the winter. Then the twigs and branches are a brilliant scarlet red—outlined against the snow, they seem to thrill with the rising sap of spring.

Edith F. Johnston

American Bittersweet or Waxwork

Flame-red and fire-orange, the fruit of the bitter-sweet burns in the tangled hedgerow or along the crumbling stone wall. The fruit is a round, orange-colored pod which divides into three parts. These three points curl back and disclose the bright scarlet seeds within. No other fruit of our wayside is as brilliant as that of the bittersweet.

The oblong leaves are a dark glossy green and grow alternately on the woody vines. The vines are very strong and often coil so tightly around a tree that they cut in through the bark until the tree is girdled and dies.

The small greenish flowers bloom in clusters in June. If you transplant the bittersweet to your garden be sure to get a fruiting vine, for the pollen-bearing flowers are on one plant and the flowers which give us the bright berries are on another.

Bittersweet berries are usually ignored by the birds until winter's alternate thawing and freezing has softened the pulp; so we can enjoy them until late in the season, often seeing them in December flaming against the snow.

Sassafras

In late summer the brilliant blue fruits of the sassafras are held up on fleshy, scarlet stems which look like little scalloped cups. But they stay only a short time on the branches, for the birds fly from far and near to strip them from the twigs.

In the North the sassafras is almost shrubby in its growth, but farther south it grows to be a tall tree with a heavy ridged bark and angular, horizontal branches.

The green-gold flowers grow in clusters. Usually the flowers having pollen are on one tree and those which are to become berries are on another. That is why we often find one tree loaded with the bright blue fruit while its neighbor is without a berry to give food to the birds.

The buds, leaves, bark, and even the roots of the sassafras have an aromatic flavor. Sassafras tea was once thought to be a remedy for many sicknesses. The Choctaw Indians of Louisiana still use the powdered leaves to give flavor to their gumbo soup.

The leaves vary in shape. Some are oval; some are two-lobed or mitten-shaped; others have three rounded lobes. Children in the country play a game with the leaves, searching for "the mitten or the double-mitten."

In autumn the foliage turns to apricot, orange, and flaming scarlet, brightening the roadsides and the old abandoned fields like gigantic bouquets of great tropical flowers.

Edith F. Johnston

Silky Dogwood

The slender branches of the silky dogwood are set with flat clusters of pale blue fruit in late summer and early autumn. They do not remain long though, for the birds are fond of them. If a band of migrating bluebirds discovers them, the bush is stripped bare in a very few minutes.

The creamy white flowers are in bloom from May to July, appearing later than those of the other dogwoods, occasionally blooming again in the autumn. Each little flower has four narrow white petals, beyond which extend four slender-stemmed stamens which give them a fuzzy look.

The young leaves are pale green and covered with a down of silky hairs. When full grown they are a bright glossy green above and silky beneath. This silky down on the underside of the oval leaves gives the shrub its name. It is also called swamp dogwood, for it is usually found in moist ground near swamps or on the edges of slow streams. The Indians called it kinnikinnick, a name they gave to any plant whose dried leaves they smoked instead of tobacco.

In autumn the silky dogwood's foliage turns to rich tones of dark crimson and deep purple. In winter, particularly as spring draws near, the branches are flushed with a reddish purple glow.

AUTUMN

Summer Grape

Virginia Creeper

Moonseed Vine

Cat Brier

Cockspur Thorn

Flowering Dogwood

Maple-leaved Viburnum

Black Alder or Winterberry

Highbush Cranberry

Black Haw

Bayberry

Summer Grape

Often forming leafy canopies or arbors as it loops from tree to tree, the summer grape is loaded with its fruits in August and September. It is a strong, woody vine climbing high on some support by means of clinging tendrils, or spreading along old fences or walls. Sometimes its strands are so heavy and strong that children make swings of them in the woods.

Wild grapes are eaten by many kinds of birds, and the wild pigeons are so fond of the fruit that in many places the vine is called pigeon grape. The fruits, small black berries with a powdery bloom, vary in size and in flavor on different vines. Some are dry and puckery; others juicy and sweet, the latter making unexcelled jelly or marmalade.

The leaves, too, vary in shape, some being so deeply cut that they are only a skeleton outline. The upper part is a dull green and beneath they are covered with cobwebby brown fuzz, sometimes in tufts along the veins.

The small greenish white flowers, coming out in clusters on the vine opposite a leaf, bloom in June. Then in the evening the air of all the lanes and byways is filled with their fragrance, one of the most exquisite scents in nature.

Edith F. Johnston

Virginia Creeper

Hanging in flowing festoons from the trees or spreading a crimson network over the rocky outcrops, the Virginia creeper, or woodbine, adds striking beauty to the edges of the woodland in early fall. We find it brightening many a bare spot from New England as far west as Texas.

The Virginia creeper belongs to the Grape Family, and so it is not surprising that its little blue-black berries are favorites of the birds. As the fruit stays on the vine nearly all winter, often robins and bluebirds live through a hard freeze, eating day by day these little berries held high above the drifting snow.

The leaves are five-parted and so can be distinguished easily from the poison ivy, which always has three leaflets. The long slender vines cling by means of tendrils which sometimes have little disks on their tips. These little disks hold tight to the support and prevent the vines from being loosened by the winds.

We hardly ever notice the large clusters of small greenish flowers. The great beauty of the Virginia creeper is in its graceful growth and brilliant scarlet autumn color.

Moonseed Vine

In rich soil at the edge of rivers or in meadow bottoms we find the luxuriant growth of the moonseed vine, loaded in autumn with its blue-black berrylike drupes very similar to the fruits of the frost grape. The hard stone in the center of the fruit is curved like a crescent moon, and this curious curved seed gives the plant its name.

The long woody strands of the moonseed clamber over low bushes and cling to dead stubs. The vines twine around and around the support or upon themselves, as they have no tendrils to help them in their growth toward the sunlight.

The large leaves, sometimes eight inches across, are smooth and bright green above and lighter below. They are a rounded oval or shield shape and are held on long slender stems which grow from almost the center of the leaf instead of from the edge.

The greenish white flowers are so small they are seldom seen. They bloom in April and May, but the fruit is not ripe until October. In America the moonseed grows wild through the Eastern states and is also often cultivated. In European gardens it has been planted to cover arbors and walls since the middle of the seventeenth century.

Edith F Johnston

Cat Brier

Studded with blue-black fruit, the vines of the cat brier form a thorny tangle on the edge of the woods or in old neglected fields. Disagreeable as its vicious thorns are to us, tearing both clothing and flesh as we explore the countryside, the spiny growth is a boon to the birds. Not only does the cat brier furnish food for the birds with its berries, but its mazelike growth makes a fortress in which their nests are safe from cats, skunks, and squirrels. The birds slip sleekly through the thorns, but their enemies dare not risk torn fur.

The cat brier grows in dry sandy soil, sending out long, spiny underground stems. The long, wirelike strands, set with hooked barbs, wind back and forth, clinging fast with tendrils. The small, greenish flowers are in clusters; those carrying pollen are on one vine, those becoming berries on another.

The leaves on different parts of the vine vary in shape, some being round, some oval, and others halberd-shaped. They are dull green above and silvery white beneath, turning to brilliant crimson and orange in the autumn. In sheltered spots in the North and in the Southern states the foliage is almost evergreen. On warm winter days we may often see a Kentucky cardinal or a mockingbird flutter to the top of a tangled growth of cat brier, then throw back his head and sing a cheerful song.

Cockspur Thorn

In October the cockspur thorn's wide-spreading branches are loaded with haws, fruits like little red crab apples. These haws often brighten the trees all winter, staying on the branches until they are eaten by the birds in the spring.

The cockspur thorn is one of the hawthorns and gets its special name because the branches are set with long, slender spines like the spurs on the feet of fighting cocks. When the trees grow in the open the long spines protect them from being eaten by cattle. The thorns also make the cockspur a good "police plant." The farmer or the gardener often plants cockspur thorns close together for hedges, and they soon grow into almost impenetrable barriers.

The hawthorns all belong to the Rose Family. The flowers of the cockspur thorn, like clusters of little apple blossoms, whiten the branches in May. Each flower has five petals set around the pink-tipped stamens.

In summer the leaves are a shiny dark green; the autumn foliage is brilliant orange and scarlet. Later the broad leafless branches catch and hold the snow, and the trees, drifted with feathery flakes, stand outlined against the blue sky as lovely as when they are covered with blossoms in spring.

Edith F. Johnston

Flowering Dogwood

The brilliant scarlet fruit of the flowering dogwood ripens in September. Hundreds of birds flock to the tree to share its bounty. The cheery song sparrow flies higher than usual to get his modest share, and even the flicker forsakes his diet of ants and grubs and excitedly loops down from his hole in a dead tree to take part in the feast.

In spring, clothed in snowy bloom, the dogwood is the loveliest tree of the open woodland. The clustered flowers are formed the summer before they bloom. All winter long they are held stiffly erect on the twigs, protected by leaves folded over them. These leaves are called bracts, and when the warm sun of April or May awakens the blossoms, the bracts break loose and soon grow large and turn white. They are like a row of snowy signaling flags waving to attract the bees to the little four-parted flowers.

The dogwood is a rather small tree, branching in circles like the spokes of a wheel. The bark is almost black and broken up into scales. The leaves grow opposite each other and are silvery green above and lighter below.

In autumn the foliage turns to rich, glowing red and orange and soft yellow. Only the upper surface of the leaves changes color, so that the tree seems to glow as if through a mist.

Edith F. Johnston

Maple-leaved Viburnum

The blue-black fruit of the maple-leaved viburnum ripens in September and gives welcome food to the birds as they fly southward. The clusters of thin-fleshed berries cling to their stems until far into the winter and many, many kinds of birds eat them. The shy hermit thrush, slipping like a shadow through the underbrush, samples them. Softly murmuring blue-birds take their share, while chattering bands of robins leave but few for the ruffed grouse and the bobwhite.

The maple-leaved viburnum grows on the edge of the forest or in the shade of the woodland. It seldom grows taller than a man's head. In May the branches are tipped with flat clusters of little creamy white flowers, each one set with five tiny white stamens.

The three-pointed leaves are shaped very much like those of the maple. They grow opposite each other on the straight branches and are reddish when they unfold, but soon become dark green. In the autumn they turn to unusual and lovely shades of old rose, dull purple, and soft lavender. In some years every leaf bleaches white before it falls and the shrub stands like a ghost among the yellow birches and flaming maples.

71

Edith F. Johnston

Black Alder or Winterberry

Even a mile away the brilliant coral-red fruits of the black alder, strung like beads on the leafless branches, catch your eye and draw you toward them as if they were magnets. The bushes usually grow in marshy ground or in the fence corner of a damp meadow, but, in spite of growing naturally in wet soil, they will grow readily in the drier soil of the garden, or at the edge of the shrubbery border.

The small, greenish white flowers bloom in May or June. They are seldom noticed, as they are hidden by the glossy green oval leaves growing alternately on the stems. The foliage turns yellow or purplish in September, soon falling and leaving the bright red berries in full view.

Because it so often grows in the marshland with the common spotted alder, this shrub is called black alder. It is also known as winterberry because we notice it more in winter than at any other time. It belongs to the Holly Family and, though it lacks the shiny evergreen leaves of the English holly of song and story, it adds cheerful color to the winter fields or the garden. In the spring its fruit is eaten greedily by cedar waxwings, robins, and bluebirds.

Highbush Cranberry

In the fall and all through the winter the highbush cranberry is loaded with its brilliant scarlet fruits, so glossy that they glint in the sunlight. The fruit is very acid and slightly bitter and, though it is sometimes cooked for sauce, it makes a poor substitute for the bog cranberry. The birds leave it severely alone until spring; then, after the fruit has been softened by winter weather, a flock of cedar waxwings or robins will make short work of the crimson harvest.

As the highbush cranberry is a viburnum, the leaves grow opposite each other on the smooth stems. When they first unfold they are reddish and downy. Later they are dull green and ridged above, and paler and downy below. In shape they are strongly three-lobed, or show three distinct points. In autumn they change to rich tints of purple and red.

The flowers, blooming in May, are in broad flat clusters. Those in the center are yellowish white, while around the edge is a circle of larger flowers, wheel-shaped and containing no stamens or pistils. These showy flowers are pure white and, like the bracts of the flowering dogwood, are there to call the attention of insects to the smaller flowers which will develop into the glossy red fruit.

The old-time snowball bush is a variety of the highbush cranberry having a round mass of these showy, sterile flowers.

Edith F. Johnston

Black Haw

When the black haw has room to spread its stout, horizontal branches on the edge of the woodland, it becomes a sturdy little tree; but we usually see it in the crowded hedgerow, where it is stunted and shrubby in shape. However, it is an obliging little tree, growing happily in the wild but also contented in the garden and even able to adapt itself to trying city conditions in parks and shaded back yards. In early autumn the fruits of the black haw cluster thick on the branches, showing green, yellow, pink, rose-red, and blue-black in the same spray. These haws are quite different from those of the hawthorn, for they are drupes—a fruit with a hard central stone covered with flesh. After they are ripe the blue-black haws hang on the branches for several months, and not until they are softened by frost are they eaten by the winter birds.

In May the rigid wide-spreading branches are so massed with pure white fragrant blossoms that they look as if covered with light drifts of snow. Each flower of the flat stemless clusters has petals in the form of a little tube with five rounded points on the edge.

As the black haw is one of the viburnums and belongs to the Honeysuckle Family, its oval leaves are set opposite each other on the twigs. They are reddish when they unfold, becoming a dark glossy green in summer. In autumn they ripen into brilliant reds and deep crimson.

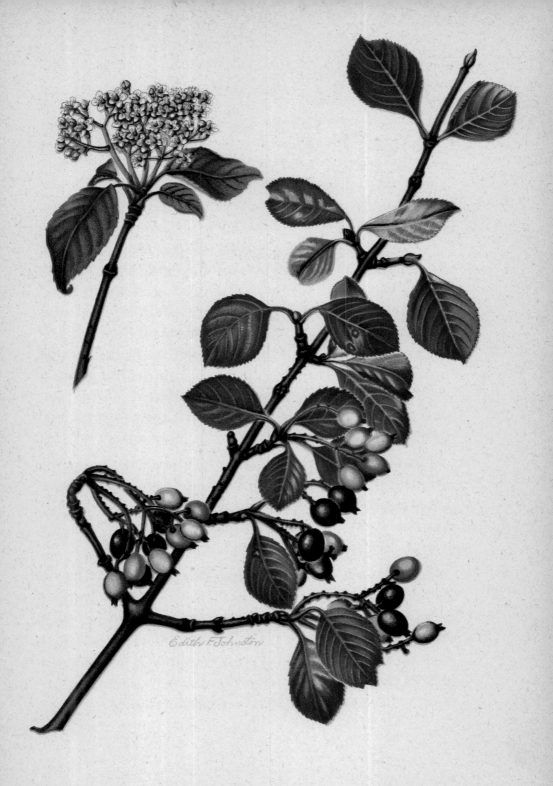

Edith F. Johnston

Bayberry

The bayberry with its dark green aromatic leaves and waxy gray berries usually grows in sandy soil, often near the seashore. In the autumn when the leaves turn bronze and fall we see clearly the clusters of fruit, strung on the branches like little pearly beads. These berries, or drupes, are made up of a hard central seed covered with dry flesh thickly coated with fragrant grayish white wax. Bayberry candles are made of this wax. The berries are boiled in water, and as the wax rises to the surface it is skimmed off and molded into candles which, as they burn, give off a sweet odor.

When the leaves of the bayberry unfurl late in spring they are coated with soft white hairs; in summer they become shiny and leathery. They are covered on both sides with tiny drops of resin, which give them their aromatic odor.

The flowers are in the form of small yellowish green catkins standing upright on the twigs. They come out at the same time as the leaves, the slender ones, bearing pollen, on one bush and the rounded ones, which produce fruit, on another.

Sometimes on the sand dunes of the Atlantic coast the bayberry bushes grow in dense thickets. Often flocks of myrtle warblers, on their way south, stay for weeks eating the waxy fruit. The bayberry not only gives food to many birds but is valuable as an anchor to hold shifting sand, or to protect more tender shrubs planted back of the thickets on the bluffs above the sea.

Edith F. Johnston

Botanical Names of Wayside Fruits

(using Bailey's *Hortus* as authority for nomenclature)

Black-Alder or Winterberry, *Ilex verticillata*
White and Red Baneberry, *Actaea alba, Actaea rubra*
Bayberry, *Myrica Pennsylvanica*
American Bittersweet, or Waxwork, *Celastrus scandens*
Climbing or Bittersweet Nightshade, *Solanum Dulcamara*
Wild Blackberry, *Rubus frondosus*
Wild Black Cherry, *Prunus serotina*
Black-haw, *Viburnum prunifolium*
Highbush Blueberry, *Vaccinium corymbosum*
Carrion-flower, *Smilax herbacea*
Cat-Brier, *Smilax glauca*
Cockspur Thorn, *Crataegus crus-galli*
Highbush Cranberry, *Viburnum Opulus var. americanum*
Virginia Creeper, *Parthenocissus quinquefolia*
Flowering Dogwood, *Cornus florida*
Red-Osier Dogwood, *Cornus stolonifera*
Silky Dogwood, *Cornus amomum*
American Elderberry, *Sambucus canadensis*
Red Elderberry, *Sambucus pubens*
Summer Grape, *Vitis aestivalis*
Japanese Honeysuckle, *Lonicera japonica var. Halliana*
Trumpet Honeysuckle, *Lonicera sempervirens*
Jack-in-the-Pulpit, *Arisaema triphyllum*
Moonseed Vine, *Menispermum canadense*
Pokeweed, *Phytolacca americana*
Blackcap Raspberry, *Rubus occidentalis*
Flowering Raspberry, *Rubus odoratus*
Rose, *var. Rosa setigera*
Sassafras, *Sassafras albidum*
Shadbush, *Amelanchier canadensis*
Snowberry and Indian Currant, *Symphoricarpos albus,
Symphoricarpos orbiculatus*
Spice-Bush, *Lindera Benzoin*
Wild Strawberry, *var. Fragaria virginiana*
Maple-leaved Viburnum, *Viburnum acerifolium*